On and off

The light is on.

The light is off.

The heater is on.

The heater is off.

The stove is on.

The stove is off.

The kettle is on.

The kettle is off.

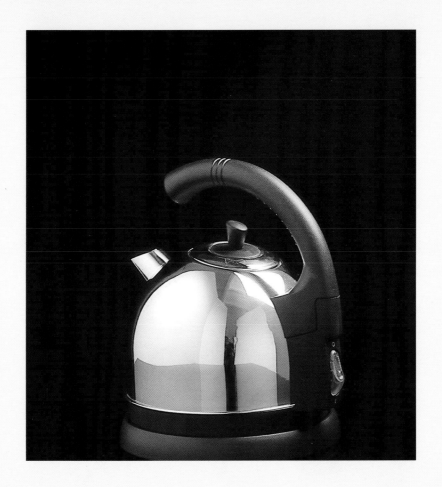

The iron is on.

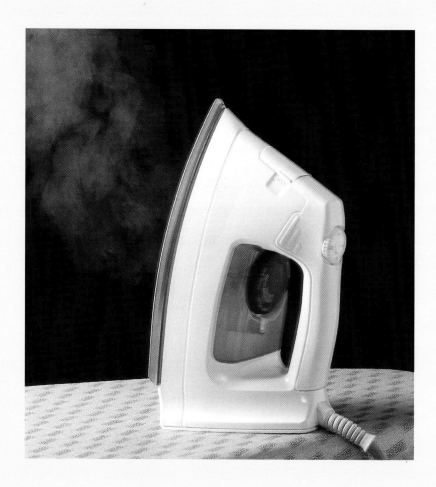

The iron is off.

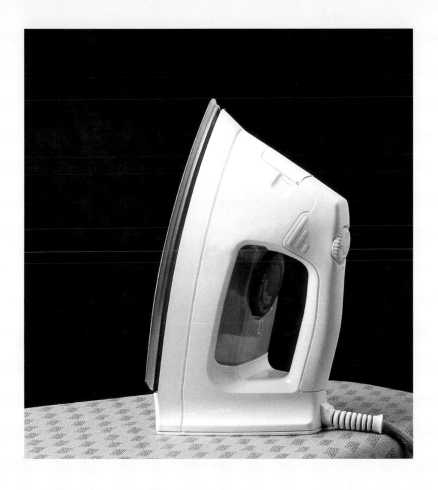

The fan is on.

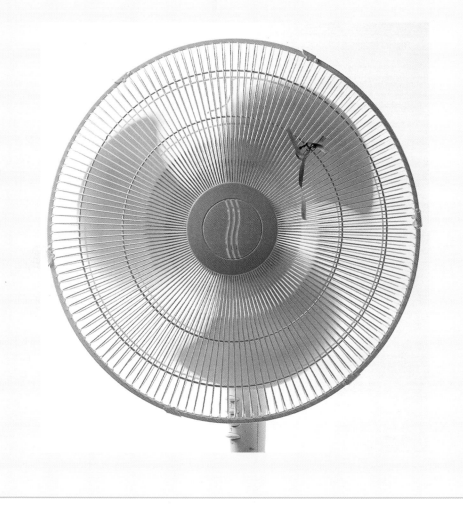

The fan is off.

The television is on.

The television is off.

The computer is on.